EPILEPSY

Susan Elliot-Wright

W

HODDER
Wayland

an imprint of Hodder Children's Books

© 2003 White-Thomson Publishing Ltd

White-Thomson Publishing Ltd,
2-3 St Andrew's Place, Lewes,
East Sussex BN7 1UP

Published in Great Britain in 2003 by Hodder Wayland, an imprint of Hodder Children's Books

This book was produced for White-Thomson Publishing Ltd by Ruth Nason.

Design: Carole Binding
Picture research: Glass Onion Pictures

The right of Susan Elliot-Wright to be identified as the author of this work has been asserted by her in accordance with the Copyright, Designs and Patents Act 1988.

British Library Cataloguing in Publication Data
Elliot-Wright, Susan
    Epilepsy. - (Health Issues)
    1. Epilepsy - Juvenile literature
    I. Title
    616.8'53

ISBN 0 7502 4380 5

Printed in Hong Kong by Wing King Tong

Hodder Children's Books
A division of Hodder Headline Limited
338 Euston Road, London NW1 3BH

Acknowledgements

The author and publishers thank the following for their permission to reproduce photographs and illustrations: Martyn Chillmaid: page 18; Corbis: cover/page 22 and pages 4 (Rob Lewine Photography), 9 (Tom Stewart Photography), 14 (Chuck Savage), 17 (Charles Gupton Photography), 21 (JFPI Studios, Inc.), 23 (Jose Luis Pelaez, Inc.), 26 (Richard T. Nowitz), 27, 31 (Little Blue Wolf Productions), 33 (Rob Lewine Photography), 34 (Ariel Skelley), 36 (Jose Luiz Pelaez), 38 (Rob Lewine/Corbis Outline), 40 (Michal Heron), 41 (Jose Luiz Pelaez), 45 (Bojan Brecelj), 48 (Richard Hutchings), 50 (Mark E. Gibson), 52 (Tom Stewart), 54 (William Taufic Photography), 55 (Natalie Fobes), 57 (Tom Stewart Photography), 59 (Phil Schermeister); Richard Greenhill: page 11; Sally Greenhill: pages 42, 47; Angela Hampton Family Life Pictures: pages 12, 49, 58; Science Photo Library: pages 6 (Juergen Berger), 24t (BSIP VEM), 24b (BSIP VEM), 25 (Jerry Mason), 28 (R. Maisonneuve), 37 (James King-Holmes). The illustrations on pages 7 and 16 are by Carole Binding.

Note: Photographs illustrating the case studies in this book were posed by models.

Every effort has been made to trace copyright holders. However, the publishers apologise for any unintentional omissions and would be pleased in such cases to add an acknowledgement in any future editions.

Contents

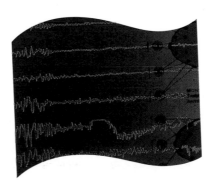

Introduction
Why should I know about epilepsy?

Epilepsy is a brain disorder, which causes people to have seizures (once called 'fits'). The brain is made up of a network of linked nerve cells, and everything we do – thinking, talking, moving – is the result of electrical signals being sent between them. The signals are sparked by chemical 'messengers'. In epilepsy, the electrical and chemical activity in the brain briefly 'goes wrong', and the messages become scrambled. It is this abnormal brain activity that causes seizures. In some cases, epilepsy is caused by damage done to the brain, for example at birth, or in an accident. But, for many, the cause is a mystery.

Many people associate epilepsy with seizures that cause the body to twitch and jerk violently, but there are many other types, depending on where in the brain the abnormal activity occurs. Chapter 1 looks at the different types of seizure and the possible causes of epilepsy.

Chapter 2 looks at what happens when someone has a seizure and how other people can help. Witnessing a seizure can be frightening, but the person experiencing it doesn't feel anything and rarely even remembers the seizure. Understanding more about seizures can help to make them less scary, whether you're the one who has epilepsy or you witness them in someone else.

Diagnosing epilepsy can be difficult, as one seizure doesn't necessarily mean epilepsy. The doctor may refer a patient

Understanding
If you or someone you know has epilepsy, it's helpful to understand as much as possible about the condition. Then it can just become a part of normal life.

who's had a seizure to a specialist. It's useful for someone who witnessed the seizure to go along too, and explain exactly what happened, as the patient probably doesn't remember. If epilepsy is suspected, specialist tests may be carried out. We look at this in Chapter 3.

Chapter 4 looks at how epilepsy is treated. The usual treatment is regular daily medication, but it can take a while to find the best drug for each individual. Eventually, most people's seizures can be reduced or even stopped by anti-epileptic drugs. Some people can gradually come off medication and remain seizure-free. For people whose seizures cannot be controlled by medication, other treatment, such as delicate brain surgery, may be an option.

'I've just changed schools so I've had to tell my new friends about my seizures because I know they can look scary. I usually feel tired and a bit strange afterwards, but I'm OK, and I don't know anything about it at the time.' (Shanna, aged 12)

It can be helpful to talk about epilepsy. In the past (and even today), epilepsy has had a 'stigma' attached. This is when people who don't understand epilepsy look down on those with the condition, causing them to be embarrassed or even ashamed, so that they try to hide their condition. These mistaken attitudes build up through lack of knowledge, and may be passed on if something is always hidden and not talked about. If you or someone you know has epilepsy, it's important to remember that epilepsy is nothing to be embarrassed about. If you are able to discuss it openly, this may help to break down some of those old ideas. If you have epilepsy, you might want to consider explaining to your friends what may trigger a seizure and what to do if one occurs. Chapter 5 looks at how your epilepsy can simply become a part of you, without anyone thinking about it.

TOWER HAMLETS COLLEGE
Learning Centre
Poplar High Street
LONDON
E14 0AF

Chapter 6 shows that people with epilepsy need to think about the effect of the condition when making choices about various things, from drinking alcohol to playing sports to choosing studies and careers. Epilepsy does not have to control a person's life, and the more we all understand the condition, the more it can be incorporated into normal, everyday life.

1 Epilepsy and the brain
Its causes and who it affects

Epilepsy is a neurological condition. This means that it is caused by something that happens in the nerve cells (neurones) of the brain. The brain is made up of millions of neurones, which are linked together. It may help to think of the brain as a computer and the neurones as wires. Neurones are responsible for controlling everything we think, feel, see, hear or do.

Electrical signals are sent along the neurones throughout the brain and into the spinal cord, where they can be relayed to other parts of the body – a sort of 'message' to that part of the body to tell it to move, breathe, swallow or whatever. These electrical messages are in the form of chemicals called neurotransmitters.

Nerve cells
Nerve cells, or neurones, allow information to be relayed rapidly around the body.

Mostly, the action of neurotransmitters is correctly balanced, but like any computer system, the brain can develop a fault or may be damaged. In epilepsy, there is sometimes an imbalance in the neurotransmitters, leading to a burst of electrical activity in the brain during which abnormal electrical signals are sent. This means the messages become jumbled up and this can lead to a seizure.

There are several different types of seizure, which fall into two main groups: partial seizures and generalized seizures. If you have epilepsy, the type of seizure you have will depend on which part of the brain is affected. For example, if the abnormal chemical activity occurs in the part that controls the function of your hand muscles, then

Frontal lobe – controls movement – seizures may include jerking, head drawn to one side and stiffness of the arm or hand.

cerebrum

Parietal lobe – associated with perception of touch – seizures may include tingling and numbness in the arm and/or leg.

Temporal lobe – many functions, including memory, speech and language, aspects of behaviour – seizures may include an odd taste or smell, strange feeling in stomach, altered behaviour or memory.

Occipital lobe – associated with vision – seizures may include visual disturbances such as flashing lights, strange colours or balls of light.

brain stem

cerebellum

your hand will twitch during the seizure. Or if the abnormal impulses are being sent right across both sides of the brain, this can lead to a generalized seizure. An epileptic seizure is also sometimes called a fit, an attack, a turn or a blackout.

Generalized seizures

The different types of seizures in this group are caused by abnormal electrical activity in both sides of the brain. They can come on with no warning, and afterwards the person cannot remember what has happened.

⬡ Tonic-clonic seizures used to be called 'grand mal'. They are the most common form of generalized seizure and what most people think of as epilepsy. The body stiffens and the person may let out a cry as they fall down unconscious. Their arms and legs start jerking and they may bite their tongue, wet themselves, grunt or foam at the mouth. During the seizure, which usually lasts a few minutes, the person may also turn blue around the mouth. This is because breathing

Areas of the brain
The type of seizure depends on the part of the brain where the jumbled messages occur.

becomes irregular during a seizure, so not enough oxygen gets into the blood. This means that the blood going to the organs (including the skin) is not as pink as usual.

After the seizure the person is often confused and tired. They may have a headache and may need sleep to recover. Some people experience only the 'tonic' phase, when the muscles stiffen, or only the 'clonic' phase, when the limbs jerk.

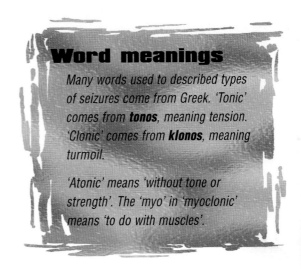

Word meanings

Many words used to described types of seizures come from Greek. 'Tonic' comes from **tonos**, meaning tension. 'Clonic' comes from **klonos**, meaning turmoil.

'Atonic' means 'without tone or strength'. The 'myo' in 'myoclonic' means 'to do with muscles'.

● Atonic seizures, or 'drop attacks', are less common. The person's muscles suddenly relax, causing them to fall heavily to the ground. Recovery is normally quick.

● Myoclonic seizures often happen within a short time of waking up and consist of brief forceful jerks of one limb or of the whole body. These seizures only last for a fraction of a second and may occur immediately before other types of generalized seizure.

● Absence seizures used to be called 'petit mal' and are most common in children and teenagers, especially girls. They are literally a brief absence of awareness. The person stops what they are doing, blinks or looks vague for a few seconds, then carries on as normal. An onlooker may either not even notice it or just think that the person is daydreaming.

'My sister has epilepsy, but before it was diagnosed, we just used to say "Cate's got the stares again". She looks like she's in another world, but afterwards she doesn't remember anything about it.' (Tom)

● Nocturnal seizures are seizures that occur during sleep. Often they are tonic-clonic or myoclonic, but they can be of other types as well. Although nocturnal means 'night-time', these seizures can happen at any time when the person is sleeping. The person will not be aware of the seizure but may wake up immediately after. They may feel tired and have a headache.

Partial seizures

These are where the abnormal activity starts in one lobe of one hemisphere of the brain. Different lobes are linked to different functions, such as memory or movement, so symptoms depend on which part of the brain is affected. There are two types of partial seizure:

- Simple partial seizures are where the person stays fully conscious and aware of what's happening. Symptoms can include strange smells or tastes, an unexplained fear, or déjà vu (the feeling that you've experienced something before). There might also be sweating, nausea or a sense of tingling and numbness in the face or an arm.

  A simple partial seizure can progress to a complex partial seizure or a generalized seizure, so these symptoms sometimes serve as an early warning. The strange feelings may last a few seconds or minutes.

'I often have complex partial seizures where I do silly things without realizing what's happening. I had one at work last week and my colleagues told me I sat in front of my computer trying to brush my hair with a pen!'
(Mike)

- Complex partial seizures are where the person's awareness or consciousness is affected. They may lose consciousness, appear dazed or confused and may carry out strange actions, known as automatisms, such as fiddling with clothes or objects,

How to help
If you are with someone who has a partial seizure, guide them away from any danger and talk to them reassuringly until they come round.

mumbling, making chewing movements, or staggering about as if they were drunk. Sometimes they do really unusual things, such as start to undress or be affectionate to strangers, without being aware of it.

Epilepsy syndromes

As well as there being different types of seizure, there are also many different types of epilepsy, known as epilepsy syndromes. A syndrome is a group of symptoms that regularly occur together. Doctors use four main pieces of information to work out which type of epilepsy syndrome someone has:

- the type of seizures they have;
- the age at which the seizures started;
- the person's learning ability;
- what is shown by an EEG (see page 24) – a special test that records electrical activity in the brain.

They also look at what is known about the possible causes, which fall into three groups:

- idiopathic – no known cause. This accounts for more than half of all people with epilepsy.
- cryptogenic – a cause is suspected, but can't be found.
- symptomatic – there is a known cause.

By looking at all this information together, the doctor may be able to use the various classifications to describe the type of epilepsy the person has. However, it varies so greatly that only around 60 per cent of people with epilepsy have a clear-cut syndrome. For example, 'idiopathic generalized tonic-clonic epilepsy': 'idiopathic' tells us that the cause is not known; 'generalized' tells us that both sides of the brain are affected; 'tonic-clonic' tells us that the seizures involve stiffness, a fall and jerking muscles.

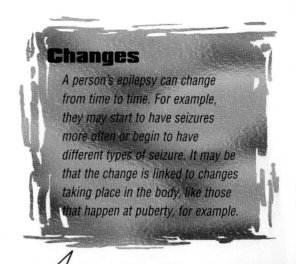

Changes

A person's epilepsy can change from time to time. For example, they may start to have seizures more often or begin to have different types of seizure. It may be that the change is linked to changes taking place in the body, like those that happen at puberty, for example.

A cycle accident

'When I was 9, I was on my bike, racing with some friends down a cycle track, when I came off and landed on my head. I wasn't wearing a cycle helmet and I hurt my head badly and was unconscious for quite a while. I stayed in hospital for nearly two weeks and I had loads of stitches. Even after I came out of hospital, I had trouble remembering things for a while. About six months later, I had my first epileptic seizure. It's not certain, but the doctors say that it is most likely that my head injury triggered my epilepsy.'
(Michelle, aged 15)

Why some people have epilepsy

For at least 6 out of 10 people who have it, epilepsy can be a mystery. Doctors don't know the cause. For the rest, it is usually that their brain either has not developed properly or has been damaged in some way, maybe as a result of infection or injury, such as in a car accident or while playing sports.

Sometimes damage to the brain occurs during pregnancy (the baby's brain doesn't develop properly) or when a baby is being born. This may happen, for example, if the baby doesn't get enough oxygen, possibly as a result of a long or difficult labour or of being born too early for the lungs to be properly developed. Damage to the brain at birth may also cause a learning disability. For a large proportion of people with learning disabilities, the damage to their brain has also caused them to have epilepsy. These kinds of problems at birth are quite a common cause of epilepsy in poorer countries around the world, but they are becoming far less common in the West, where there is better hospital care.

'Over half of our 18 clients also have epilepsy, though only three have frequent seizures. Some of them understand their epilepsy well, and we talk about it, which helps.'
(June, learning disabilities day care worker)

Epilepsy is not, as some people think, linked to intelligence. It can occur in people with average, above average or below average intelligence. However, it is more common in people who have learning disabilities, people whose brains haven't developed properly or who have suffered brain damage, and people who have certain conditions that affect the brain. These include meningitis (an inflammation of the lining of the brain); encephalitis (a virus affecting the brain); cerebral palsy (a brain abnormality); and brain abscesses. Brain tumours are a rare cause of epilepsy in adults. Epilepsy may also occur in older people with conditions such as dementia (a mental disorder with a variety of causes) or those who have had a stroke (where there is a temporary interruption in the blood supply to the brain).

Who gets epilepsy?

Epilepsy is the most common serious neurological, or brain, disorder and affects 50 million people around the world. In the UK, 350,000 people have the condition – that's about 1 in 200 people. It is most common in children and teenagers, and in people over 65.

Granddad's blackouts

Ian's granddad is 70, and he got epilepsy after a mild stroke. 'I didn't really know what to expect and I was scared the first time I saw Granddad have a seizure. I thought he was going to die! He suddenly looked strange, staring into thin air. Then he collapsed and started frothing at the mouth and jerking. I was glad Mum was there. She just knelt down with him and made sure he didn't hurt himself. After about two minutes he seemed to come round, although he had to go and lie down. He's got tablets from the hospital now, and they seem to keep it under control. He only has seizures occasionally – he calls them his blackouts – and it doesn't stop him doing his garden.'

Any person's brain can produce a seizure in certain situations, but normally, the brain has a natural threshold below which a seizure will not happen. Some things can lower that threshold, for example: brain tumours or infections, drugs, alcohol, diabetes. If the thing that lowers the 'seizure threshold' is permanently present, seizures will be repeated and the person will have epilepsy.

Febrile convulsions

Children under 5 sometimes have febrile convulsions. These are a type of seizure that may happen when a child has a high temperature. Febrile convulsions are not epilepsy and are nearly always harmless. However, a child who has had them has a slightly higher chance of developing epilepsy later on.

Epilepsy is most likely to develop in childhood or the early teens, but around a third of people who develop it before they are 16 will 'grow out of it' by the time they reach adulthood. The age at which they have their last seizure will vary, like most aspects of epilepsy, from person to person.

The second most common age group to get epilepsy is the over-60s. This is because older people are more likely to have health problems such as strokes, which can damage the brain.

Can epilepsy be inherited?

Research suggests that some of the many different types of epilepsy may have a genetic basis. Genes are the parts of a human cell that determine the characteristics you inherit from your parents, such as brown eyes, a small nose or big feet. It may be that an abnormal gene can cause some types of epilepsy, so, if someone inherits that abnormal gene from their parents, then they may develop epilepsy.

It may also be that some people inherit a low seizure threshold (also part of their genetic make-up); therefore something would trigger a seizure in them that wouldn't be enough to trigger a seizure in someone else. However, even if you carry the abnormal gene or if you have inherited a low seizure threshold, you will not necessarily develop epilepsy.

2 Understanding seizures
What to do if one occurs

Living with seizures

Epilepsy is not the same for everyone. There are many different types of epilepsy and many different types of seizures. Some people have several seizures a day, while others go for years without one. For some people, anti-epileptic drugs prevent seizures completely. Others still have some seizures, though fewer and less severe than if they had not been on medication.

Someone's experiences of epilepsy can also vary depending on how their family and friends react. Parents, for example, may become over-protective because they're worried about how their child will cope with the condition. (More about this in Chapter 6.)

'A lady at the hospital said she has complex partial seizures too. But she gets dazed and looks drunk, and I do weird things without realizing. The doctor said seizures are all different, depending on where in the brain they start.' (Lara, aged 15)

Warning signs and auras

Some people with epilepsy, though not all, experience a warning that a seizure is about to happen. They may feel unusually anxious, notice a strange taste or smell, feel odd sensations in the stomach or tingling in the limbs, have a sense of déjà vu, or they may see or hear strange things. This is called having an 'aura'. An aura is actually a brief 'mini' seizure, caused by the stirrings of activity in the brain that will eventually become a seizure.

Seizures can happen anywhere and at any time, even in your sleep, and a person can have more than one type. Many people find that the type of seizures they have, how often they happen and how long they last tend to stay the same. However, the pattern may change for a variety of reasons, including the effects of anti-epileptic drugs or hormonal changes, such as those that occur during puberty. Some people stop having seizures in their teens; for others, this is when seizures start. Any change in seizures should be reported, so that the doctor can decide if the treatment needs to be changed.

Up to 80 per cent of people with epilepsy find that the right medication stops their seizures completely. However, it can take a long time to find the 'right' medication. Most people go through a period of trying out various drugs to see which is best for them. For some people, it's not possible to control their seizures completely. Others choose not to take anti-epileptic drugs because of side effects or because they don't have seizures very often.

'I worried epilepsy would ruin my life. It took two years to find a drug that suited me, but it works so well that I hardly ever have seizures now. I'm so glad I could take up swimming again. It's my favourite sport!'
(Kerry, aged 19)

How people can help

When someone has epilepsy, it helps if they can talk about their condition with their family and friends. Understanding what happens during a seizure and how to deal with one if it occurs makes people more relaxed about epilepsy.

If you're worried about spending time with someone who has epilepsy, ask if they would mind telling you something about it. It could be useful for you to know what type of seizures they have, how long they normally last, what usually triggers them, and how often they happen. This will help you know what to do if they have a seizure while you are there.

Witnessing a seizure

Most seizures happen without warning, last only a short time and stop without the person needing any special treatment. Injuries can occur, but usually a seizure isn't a medical emergency and the person won't come to any harm. Even so, watching someone have a seizure can be distressing or even frightening. They may behave in a strange way, appear to be in a trance or their body may be moving around and twitching uncontrollably. You need to

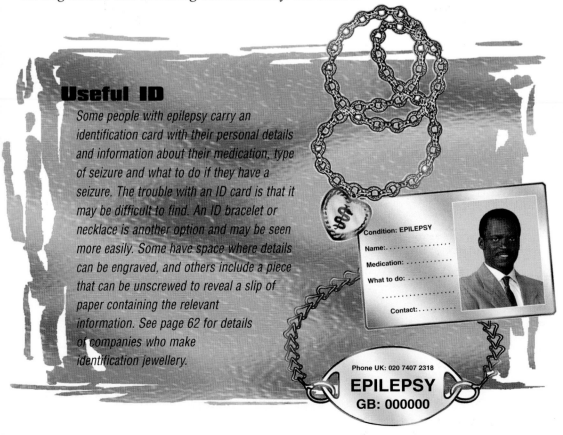

Useful ID

Some people with epilepsy carry an identification card with their personal details and information about their medication, type of seizure and what to do if they have a seizure. The trouble with an ID card is that it may be difficult to find. An ID bracelet or necklace is another option and may be seen more easily. Some have space where details can be engraved, and others include a piece that can be unscrewed to reveal a slip of paper containing the relevant information. See page 62 for details of companies who make identification jewellery.

Condition: EPILEPSY

Name:. . . . .

Medication: . . . .

What to do: . . . .

. . . .

Contact:. . . . .

Phone UK: 020 7407 2318

EPILEPSY
GB: 000000

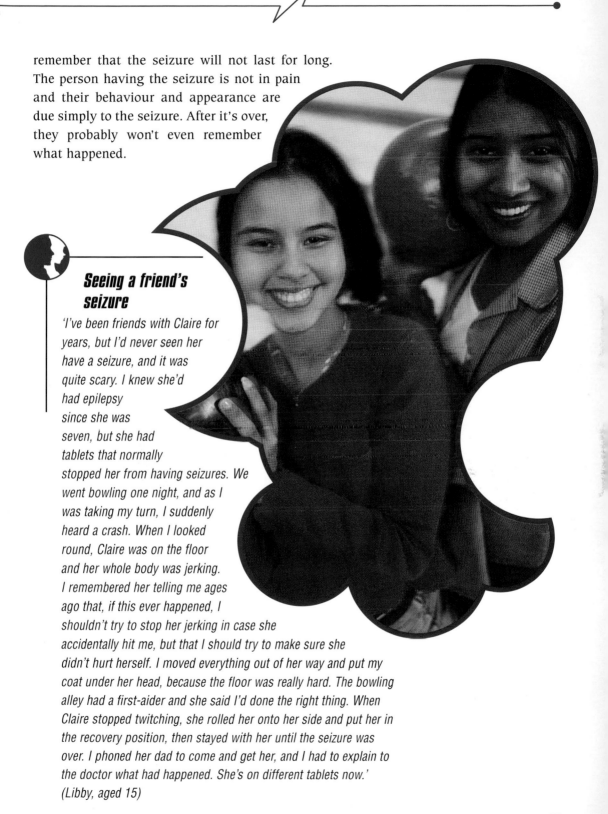

remember that the seizure will not last for long. The person having the seizure is not in pain and their behaviour and appearance are due simply to the seizure. After it's over, they probably won't even remember what happened.

Seeing a friend's seizure

'I've been friends with Claire for years, but I'd never seen her have a seizure, and it was quite scary. I knew she'd had epilepsy since she was seven, but she had tablets that normally stopped her from having seizures. We went bowling one night, and as I was taking my turn, I suddenly heard a crash. When I looked round, Claire was on the floor and her whole body was jerking. I remembered her telling me ages ago that, if this ever happened, I shouldn't try to stop her jerking in case she accidentally hit me, but that I should try to make sure she didn't hurt herself. I moved everything out of her way and put my coat under her head, because the floor was really hard. The bowling alley had a first-aider and she said I'd done the right thing. When Claire stopped twitching, she rolled her onto her side and put her in the recovery position, then stayed with her until the seizure was over. I phoned her dad to come and get her, and I had to explain to the doctor what had happened. She's on different tablets now.'
(Libby, aged 15)

How to help if someone has a tonic-clonic seizure

A person having a tonic-clonic seizure may do some or all of the following: suddenly go stiff, fall over, turn blue, make jerking movements, cry out or foam at the mouth. However, they should soon be fine and won't normally need medical help. Here are some dos and don'ts.

If someone has a tonic-clonic seizure ...

DO ✔

- Try not to panic. You can't stop a seizure and the person should recover fully.
- Notice how long the seizure lasts. If it's more than a few minutes the person might need medical help.
- Put something soft under the person's head, and move hard or sharp objects out of the way.
- Loosen clothing around the neck.
- When the jerking stops, roll the person into the recovery position. Stay with them until they have recovered fully.
- Check for any injuries and seek medical advice if necessary.

DON'T ✘

- Move them – unless they're in a dangerous place such as at the top of some stairs or in the road.
- Try to stop the jerking. This could hurt them or you.
- Put anything in their mouth or force anything between their teeth to stop them swallowing their tongue. A person having a seizure cannot swallow their tongue, and putting something in their mouth might choke them or damage their teeth.

Recovery position

Putting someone in the recovery position (lying them on their left side, with their right arm and right leg bent) helps them to breathe normally again.

How to help people with other types of seizure

- **Complex partial seizure**: the person seems confused, wanders around as if they were dazed or drunk, and doesn't seem aware of what they are doing. Guide them away from danger, such as a busy road or staircase, and talk gently to them to help them come round.

- **Simple partial seizure**: the person experiences strange feelings, which can be upsetting, so stay with them and talk reassuringly to them while the seizure lasts. Also, remember that a simple partial seizure may become a complex partial or generalized one.

- **Tonic and atonic seizures**: the person falls down, then recovers quickly. Check for any injuries and stay with them until they are fully recovered.

- **Absence seizures**: the person has brief interruptions of awareness, as if they were daydreaming. You can help by guiding them away from any danger.

After a seizure

After a seizure, some people need to rest or sleep for a few hours to recover fully. Others can carry on as normal. If you have epilepsy, make sure you give yourself time to recover and get any injuries checked out by a doctor.

When it's an emergency

There is usually no need to call an ambulance, but you should call for one if:

- it is the person's first seizure;

- the person is injured during a seizure, or may have breathed in water;

- the person has problems breathing after a seizure;

- a seizure goes on for an unusually long time or the person has two or more seizures without regaining consciousness.

Status epilepticus

A person's seizures tend to last for the same amount of time, usually a few seconds or minutes, and stop on their own. But seizures can last 30 minutes or more. Having seizures lasting more than 30 minutes, or experiencing several seizures without a break and lasting a total of 30 minutes or more is called 'status epilepticus'. This is an emergency and needs immediate medical attention and special medication.

3 How do they know it's epilepsy?
Getting a diagnosis

No one test can prove or disprove that someone has epilepsy, and there are several possible reasons for seizures. Epilepsy is a tendency to have *recurrent* seizures, but one person in 20 has a *single* seizure at some time in their life. That is why, if someone goes to their doctor because they have had a seizure or because they seem to have had one, the doctor won't always immediately carry out tests for epilepsy; they may wait to see if another seizure happens.

When it's not epilepsy

There are some conditions where the symptoms are similar to those seen in epilepsy. For this reason, conditions such as syncope (fainting), migraine, hyperventilation and 'pseudo-seizures' can sometimes be confused with epilepsy. In children, breath-holding attacks and night terrors may be mistaken for epilepsy.

'I fainted five times in two weeks. It must have been the summer heat, or a virus. Apparently, my body twitched as I fell. My doctor referred me to the hospital, but I was fine again when I saw the specialist. She said it didn't sound like epilepsy.'
(Jess, aged 16)

⊚ Syncope is the medical term for fainting, and happens when the brain doesn't get enough blood due to the heart rate slowing down. People sometimes faint if they've had a shock, have very bad pain, or if they have been standing for a long time in a hot enclosed space. When someone faints, their body may jerk slightly, which is why fainting is sometimes confused with an epileptic seizure.

⊚ A migraine is a severe, throbbing headache, often on one side of the head and often accompanied by nausea, tingling or numbness in the face and arms, and 'visual disturbances' such as bright lights, blurred vision or seeing a 'halo' around objects. These effects can be confused with those of a simple partial seizure, especially as it's not unusual to have a splitting headache after a seizure.

⊛ Hyperventilation (breathing too hard or too fast) is not uncommon in people who are very stressed or who have panic attacks. Over-breathing reduces the levels of carbon dioxide in the blood and may cause tingling sensations, light-headedness and even blackouts.

⊛ Pseudo-seizures are difficult to tell from real epileptic seizures. These attacks are not real seizures, in that they have a psychological rather than a physical or chemical cause, but the person still has little control over them. They may fall, appear to lose consciousness, and then thrash around or lie motionless. Little is known about the cause of pseudo-seizures, but it is thought they may be linked to emotional problems or trauma, such as bereavement, divorce or physical or sexual abuse.

⊛ Breath-holding attacks usually affect toddlers, often as part of a temper tantrum. The child holds his/her breath until s/he passes out. The child may turn blue due to lack of oxygen and this, together with the loss of consciousness, can suggest epilepsy.

⊛ Night terrors usually affect children of around three and over. Unlike nightmares, which usually occur during light sleep and often wake the child up, night terrors occur during the deepest period of sleep. Although the child may appear to wake, may have their eyes open, and may scream as if terrified, they do not actually wake and therefore cannot be comforted. The child remembers nothing the next day. It is this apparently strange behaviour and loss of awareness while appearing to be awake that can result in night terrors being confused with epilepsy.

Migraine attack
Several of the symptoms of migraine are similar to those of a partial seizure.

What the doctor needs to know

To be able to distinguish between epilepsy and non-epileptic attacks, the doctor needs detailed information about the seizure. Often the person affected does not remember what happened, so it helps for a friend or parent to describe the seizure to the doctor. Although seeing a seizure can be frightening, it's important to remember as much as possible so that you can provide clues to help with the diagnosis.

'I went with Mum and my sister Milly to see the epilepsy doctor. I told him how Milly's arms and legs had started twitching, and her face went a funny colour. She looked awake, but didn't remember anything afterwards.'
(Linton, aged 11)

One of the most important factors in diagnosing epilepsy is the question and answer session with the doctor. The doctor asks about the person's medical history to see whether there is or has been any other condition, illness or injury that may be relevant. In an older person, for example, the doctor might want to see whether the person has had a mild stroke, which may have caused epilepsy. Then there will be questions about the seizure itself. This is where the witness comes in, as they will probably be able to provide much more information than the person who had the seizure.

Information

The doctor needs as much information as possible, about how the person felt before and after the seizure, and what the seizure looked like.

If epilepsy is suspected, the doctor may want to rule out other possible causes before referring the person to a hospital specialist. The specialist will then carry out a number of other tests and investigations to help diagnose the problem.

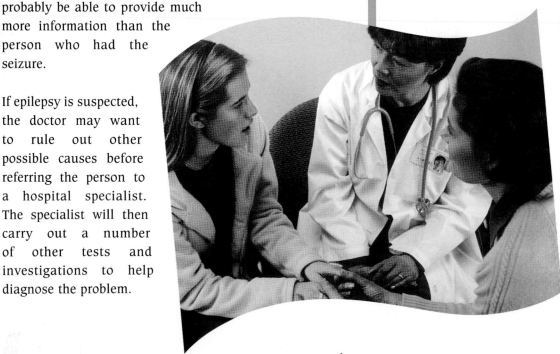

Finding out if it's epilepsy

'Matthew came to my surgery with his mother, after he'd collapsed following football practice. Another of my patients, Peter, came with them. His lad and Matthew are chums. Peter said he'd seen similar episodes in a colleague who has epilepsy, but of course the nature of seizures, and of epilepsy itself, can vary enormously, so I wanted to gather lots of information before I referred Matthew to the hospital.

As he's only 11, I got his mum to tell me about his medical history. I asked whether he'd been born early, or whether labour had been long or difficult. But Matthew was a healthy baby, born after a straightforward labour and delivery, so it's unlikely there's any brain damage we don't know about. Matthew hadn't had any head injuries, but he'd had suspected meningitis when he was two. I made a note to check his records and pass this on to the hospital – it could be relevant, and the specialist will need to know everything. Diagnosing epilepsy is a bit like doing a jig-saw – all the pieces have to fit.

Matthew couldn't remember anything about the seizure, except that he'd felt "strange" just before. He mentioned a funny sensation in his stomach, which could be significant as a seizure starting in the brain's temporal lobe can affect the stomach.

Peter was very helpful in describing Matthew's seizure. He confirmed that Matthew had complained of a nasty feeling in his stomach a few minutes beforehand. I asked what Matthew had been doing before the seizure – sometimes this can be relevant in working out what triggered it. We also need to know how the seizure appeared – whether there was any stiffness or twitching, whether Matthew made any noise, whether his breathing changed and so on. I also asked how long the seizure lasted and how Matthew was afterwards. Peter gave a very clear picture of Matthew's seizure. He described several possible epilepsy symptoms. I'll definitely refer Matthew to the hospital, and I'll send them a full report of what happened.'
(Dr Jim Howard, Matthew's family doctor)

Medical tests

A sample of blood may be taken and sent away to be analysed at a laboratory. The blood can be tested to check the person's overall health, and look for other conditions, such as diabetes, that could explain the seizure.

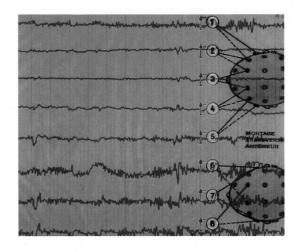

An EEG (electroencephalogram) is a test that records the brain's activity. Electrodes are attached to the head to pick up the electrical signals (brainwaves) between nerve cells in the brain. These signals are amplified and recorded onto paper or displayed on a TV screen. The recording is a picture (called a 'trace') of the brainwaves being produced by different parts of the brain, depending on where the electrodes are placed. A 'normal' trace shows slightly wiggly lines in a fairly regular pattern. In someone with epilepsy, the lines may show unusual brainwave patterns, called 'seizure discharges', which may look wavy or spiky, and may be irregular in shape. These patterns can help the doctors work out where the abnormal signals are occurring, and how frequently.

Picturing brain activity

EEG traces are pictures of the brainwaves produced by different parts of the brain. The trace above shows normal brainwaves. Below is a trace of brainwaves during an epileptic seizure.

However, an EEG only gives information about the brain's activity during the period of recording. If no abnormalities are found, this doesn't necessarily mean that the person doesn't have epilepsy – only that the abnormalities weren't showing when the test was carried out. Many people with epilepsy have normal EEGs between seizures. An EEG can only confirm a diagnosis of epilepsy if the person actually has a seizure during the EEG – so sometimes the doctor will suggest attempting to bring on a seizure so that a more effective EEG can be carried out. This can be done by encouraging the patient to

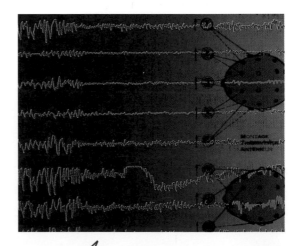

Tests, but no proof

'I had a funny turn so my mum took me to the doctor. He said I'd better see a specialist at the hospital to test whether I might have epilepsy. At the hospital, I had an EEG. Lots of electrodes, or wires, were stuck to my scalp to record my brainwaves. Then the operator showed me lights and shapes to try to provoke abnormal brain patterns.

I also had a scan, which meant I had to lie on a bed with lots of hi-tech machinery around me, taking pictures of my brain. When we saw the specialist two weeks later, she explained that the tests hadn't proved anything, but she was pretty sure my symptoms showed I had epilepsy. She started me on some pills that should control it, and gave us loads of leaflets about epilepsy.' (Clare, aged 14)

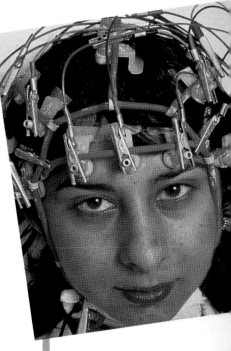

EEG electrodes
Signals picked up by the electrodes produce a trace of the person's brainwaves, like those shown on page 24.

hyperventilate (breathe very quickly) or by using other potential triggers. (More about triggers in Chapter 5.)

If someone with suspected epilepsy has a 'normal' reading from a routine EEG, doctors may suggest a further specialized EEG. It's quite common to have several different EEGs to help doctors gather the information they need. These may include:

- ambulatory monitoring – this means monitoring while walking around. Electrodes are attached to the head and connected to a portable unit worn over the shoulder or round the waist. Brainwaves are recorded onto a special 24-hour cassette tape and the person keeps a written record of their activities and how they feel. A button on the unit can be pressed, either by the patient or by someone with them, if they think a seizure might be starting. This highlights that area of the tape, to help doctors pinpoint what was happening when the abnormal brain activity began. At the end of the test, special equipment is used to convert the information on the tape into a standard EEG trace.

● videotelemetry – this links a video camera to an EEG machine so that it records both the electrical activity in the person's brain and what they are doing at the time. The screen simultaneously shows what is happening to the patient (the clinical evidence) and the EEG recording. If the video records someone having an attack while the EEG is normal, it is likely that the person does not have epilepsy. With this type of test the person can be observed for a longer period, during which a seizure is more likely. Also, as the test acts as an eyewitness to a seizure, it can help determine the type of epilepsy. It is often used to assess people who are being considered for surgery.

Brain scans

A brain scan may be carried out to see if there is a physical cause for a person's seizures, such as damage to an area of the brain caused by a head injury. A CT or CAT (computed tomography) scan is a type of X-ray, for which the patient lies with their head still in a scanner for a few minutes. Information from the scanner is sent to a computer, which displays the X-ray as a series of pictures of slices of the skull and brain.

MRI (Magnetic Resonance Imaging) scanning, which is replacing CT scans, gives clearer, more detailed pictures and can detect even very small abnormalities. The downside is that the patient must lie still inside the cylinder of the scanner for around 30 minutes, and some people find this a little unpleasant. MRI scans are especially good for assessing a patient's suitability for surgery.

MRI brain scan

For an MRI scan, the person must lie still inside the scanner for 30 minutes or so. As MRI scanning develops, it is becoming more and more possible to pinpoint the part of the brain where seizures are beginning.

Reactions to diagnosis

Being told that you or someone close to you has epilepsy can be a shock. You may feel angry, anxious or sad. Some people become depressed. For others, it's a relief to know what's been causing their attacks, and they are glad to start treatment.

The diagnosis can change the way you feel about yourself and the way that others see you. Sadly, epilepsy still carries a stigma and some people wrongly associate it directly with mental illness or learning problems. For this reason, some people hide the fact that they have epilepsy. If you have epilepsy, you need to decide whom to tell. You may feel uncomfortable about this, and prefer not to discuss it. On the other hand, if you do feel you want to talk about it, this may help people to understand epilepsy and go some way towards getting rid of mistaken ideas.

Talking to your doctor, specialist nurses, counsellors and people on epilepsy charity helplines may help when you are coming to terms with the diagnosis. They can also tell you about local self-help groups. Some websites have chat rooms for teenagers. Whatever you decide to do, remember it's your choice. It also helps to remember that most people with epilepsy can, and do, lead full and active lives.

Chat room

Some people find it helpful to talk about their epilepsy to someone they don't know – for example, via a chat room on an epilepsy website.

No great change

'I was upset when I was told I had epilepsy. I read the leaflets they gave me and got some books from the library. They said things like I shouldn't drink too much, I shouldn't lock the bathroom door, I shouldn't stay out late clubbing or get too tired, and I might not be able to drive. At 17, I was just getting to the age when I could have real fun and now it seemed as if my life was over. Fortunately, the pills I was given seemed to get my seizures under control very quickly, and after a few months things didn't seem so bad. As long as I'm careful, I can do most things my friends do, and I've met some other young people with epilepsy through a club. My life didn't change anywhere near as much as I feared.' (Andrew, aged 20)

4 Treating epilepsy
Finding the best way to prevent seizures

There is no cure for epilepsy, but the good news is that many anti-epileptic drugs are now available which can control the condition and prevent the person from having seizures. For around 60-70 per cent of people with epilepsy, one drug controls their seizures completely. For another 10 per cent, taking a combination of two drugs is effective. Some of the other 20-30 per cent choose not to take medication, perhaps because their seizures only happen very infrequently or because they prefer to avoid the side effects. For some whose epilepsy is not controlled by drugs, brain surgery may now be an option. Research is constantly going on to find even better treatments. All this means that having epilepsy nowadays is completely different from the way it was for people in the past.

Drug research
Research is going on all the time to develop drugs that control seizures, without side effects.

How epilepsy was treated in the past

The earliest references to people having epilepsy date back thousands of years. In ancient times, people thought that seizures were caused by evil spirits and that the person was 'possessed' by demons. Writing on a Babylonian tablet from 2000 BC describes many of the seizure types we recognize today, attributing each type to a different spirit or god. Treatment in those days was spiritual rather than physical, and priests were called in to treat the person with prayers or magic.

In 400 BC, this superstition was challenged by great physicians such as Atreya of India and Hippocrates of Greece. Both argued that what was called 'the falling sickness' or 'the sacred disease' was not supernatural, but was in fact a dysfunction of the brain.

Recommended treatments included eating mistletoe, having enemas and purges, and taking blood. People in Julius Caesar's time who were thought to have epilepsy were often seen sucking blood from fallen gladiators.

'If you will cut open the head, you will find the brain humid, full of sweat and having a bad smell. And this is the way truly you may see that it is not God that injures the body, but disease.' (Hippocrates, c.460–c.377 BC)

Opinion continued to be divided on the causes of epilepsy. Around the fifteenth century, the evil spirit theory was popular again. Sufferers were accused of sorcery and punished by being burned alive. The view that epilepsy was a brain disorder wasn't really accepted until the nineteenth century, and even then, strange opinions and treatments were common. The nineteenth-century poet Alfred Lord Tennyson had 'waking trances' which are thought to have been epilepsy. The treatment he underwent involved drinking large amounts of water, walking long distances in bad weather and being wrapped in sheets and dunked into cold baths.

Throughout this time, people with epilepsy suffered huge social stigma. They were often feared, misunderstood and shunned by the people around them. It is this long-standing misconception that has led to the stigma that persists among some people even today.

The beginning of modern treatments

Modern treatments were introduced as the idea of brain disorder became more accepted. In 1873, a neurologist called Hughlings Jackson suggested that seizures were the result of abnormal electrical discharges in the brain, and that the character of the seizure depended on the location of those discharges. However, it wasn't until the 1920s that the EEG was developed. This enabled doctors to see how brainwave patterns indicated different types of seizures. It also opened up possibilities for surgical treatments, which became more widely available from around the 1950s.

The first effective anti-epileptic drug was bromide. It was widely used in Europe and the USA throughout the late nineteenth and early twentieth centuries. Other drugs used in the first half of the twentieth century were phenobarbitone, introduced in 1912, and phenytoin, introduced in 1938. Since the 1960s, greater understanding of the brain's activity has led to the rapid discovery and development of more effective drugs, with fewer side effects.

The use of anti-epileptic drugs today

Many anti-epileptic drugs are available today. Doctors do not know exactly how all the drugs work. Some seem to correct chemical imbalances in the brain and others help reduce the abnormal brain activity that causes seizures. Nor do they know why some drugs work for some people, but not for others. Some of the drugs are more effective for certain types of epilepsy. Some give one person side effects, while another person can use them without any problems. Some anti-epileptic drugs can even make certain forms of epilepsy worse. For all these reasons, when someone has been diagnosed with epilepsy, their doctor needs to try them on different drugs in order to find the one that controls their seizures best with the least number of side effects.

Getting the treatment right can take a while. The doctor usually prescribes a low dose of a drug at first and builds it up slowly so there is less chance of side effects. It takes time for a drug to reach the necessary levels in the bloodstream. Progress is monitored and, if the person's seizures aren't controlled, the doctor may increase the dose, change the

Why drugs must be taken regularly

For a drug to work properly, it must be built up to a certain level in the person's blood and be kept at that level by taking regular doses. This is necessary because, once medicines have travelled around the bloodstream, they leave the body, either by being broken down (metabolized) or by being passed in urine. Some drugs need to be taken 3-4 times a day, others only once a day, in order to keep levels steady.

Epilepsy can change

'When my epilepsy was diagnosed, I tried three different drugs before we got to one that worked. It was brilliant for a while – I only had three seizures in two years. But then they started to come more often, although they were different from before – not quite as severe. First it was every couple of months, then every three weeks, and in the last six weeks I've had four seizures. I had loads of arguments with my mum, because she thought I wasn't taking my medication. In the end, she insisted on watching while I swallowed my pills, so it proved I wasn't lying.

I saw my doctor last week, and he said that sometimes your epilepsy changes and you need a different drug. He said it might be to do with my age. He's prescribed some new tablets and, so far, I haven't had another seizure. I'll have to wait and see. The doctor said that, if this drug doesn't work, there are more we can try, so I'm not too worried.'
(James, aged 15)

drug or try a combination of drugs. Some people are lucky and the first drug they try is right for them. Others have to try several different drugs and the process of finding the best treatment can take months or even over a year.

During the period of getting the treatment right, a person with epilepsy needs to see their doctor regularly, for blood tests to check the levels of the drug in their blood, and to discuss how well the treatment is working. After the treatment is sorted out, the person must still visit their doctor or hospital regularly, although not as often, for the treatment to be reviewed.

'After I started medication I didn't have any more seizures – until I got a stomach bug! The doctor said it was probably because the drugs hadn't "stayed in my body".'
(Rachel, aged 15)

Sometimes seizures can be controlled for several months, but then start again. This could happen if the person doesn't take their drugs properly, or if they find they need a larger dose, or as a result of illness.

Sometimes a person's epilepsy changes and they need to try a different drug, or they may want to stop taking drugs altogether if they have been seizure-free for a long time. All these are reasons why someone with epilepsy should see their doctor for further advice. It's also important for anyone on epilepsy medication to be monitored by their doctor when they start to take the contraceptive Pill, as these two drugs can make each other less effective.

Taking the medicine

Anti-epileptic drugs are taken by mouth and most come in different forms, such as tablets or pills, capsules, liquids and powders (which are used by dissolving them in drinks). This means that everyone should be able to choose a form of medication that suits them. The drugs must be prescribed by a doctor, and in the UK, the person with epilepsy does not have to pay for them.

Anti-epileptic drugs, like all drugs, have a chemical or scientific name and a brand or trade name, which is given by the pharmaceutical company that makes the drug. If a drug is made by more than one company, it may have more than one brand name. Doctors normally tell their patients the brand name of the drug they are prescribing and get them to stick to this. This is because research has shown that different brands of the same drug are absorbed at different rates by the body. If someone changes brands, the level of the drug in their bloodstream could be lowered so much that it no longer prevents seizures. If you take drugs for epilepsy and you travel abroad, remember that different brand names are used in other countries.

Taking care about mixing drugs

If you take any type of medication regularly (including anti-epileptic drugs), you should be careful about taking other drugs at the same time. Different drugs interact with each other: the absorption of any of the drugs may be changed, their potency may be reduced or increased, or the combination of drugs may cause side effects. Always check with the pharmacist that other medicines will be suitable for you.

Who needs to know?

Doctors, dentists and any other health workers treating a person with epilepsy for another problem or illness need to know about the person's epilepsy and about any anti-epileptic medication they take. This is so that they can decide on the best way to treat the person, without upsetting the balance of anti-epileptic drugs in their bloodstream and without causing unpleasant side effects. It's also possible that the person's illness may make a seizure more likely.

In an emergency, a person with epilepsy may not be able to give information about their own condition and medication. That is why many people choose to carry some form of medical ID (see page 16).

Drowsiness
A common side effect of anti-epileptic drugs is to make you feel very sleepy. You should tell your doctor if this or any other side effect is a problem.

Side effects

All drugs can cause side effects, even the aspirin or paracetamol you take for a headache or a cold. The first anti-epileptic drugs tended to have unpleasant side effects. Bromide, for example, is rarely used today. Drugs such as phenobarbitone and phenytoin were popular before the Second World War, but these 'older' drugs still tend to have more side effects than those developed in the last 10 or 20 years. Doctors usually prescribe these newer drugs first, moving on to the older drugs if they don't work. They may also try drugs developed in the 1960s and 1970s, such as sodium valproate and carbamazepine, which usually have fewer side effects than the older drugs, but a few more than the newer drugs.

Some people don't experience any side effects from their anti-epileptic drugs. Others notice only minor problems, which calm down or disappear after a few weeks. For example, many people with epilepsy find that their drugs make them sleepy at first, but this often passes as their body gets used to the drug. Some people have an allergic reaction to the drugs and this may result in an itchy, possibly severe skin rash. Rarely, an allergic reaction can cause liver or kidney problems.

Side effects are more likely if a drug is started at a high dose, if the dose is increased too quickly, or if a person needs to take two or more anti-epileptic drugs at the same time. Common side effects include dizziness, drowsiness, poor concentration, headache and upset stomach. Less common side effects are swollen gums, acne, weight gain, hirsutism (hairiness), hair loss, hyperactivity (in children), depression or even psychosis, a serious mental health problem. These are more common in people who have to take the drugs, especially the 'older' types, for a long time.

Medication and moods

Sally, aged 15, started taking epilepsy drugs when she was nine, but they made her feel odd and affected the way she behaved. 'I was on them for several months,' she recalls, 'but they didn't work well – I still had several seizures a week, and I became moody and depressed. My mum thought the medication was to blame, because I wasn't usually like that. She took me back to the specialist, who suggested changing the drug.' Since then Sally has been much better. 'Now instead of having several seizures a week, I only have one when I'm tired or feeling run-down. And my moods have completely changed. I'm much happier and argue a lot less with my parents.'

If side effects become troublesome, the doctor will probably lower the dose or change the drug. Some people choose to put up with minor side effects, because they decide this is better than having seizures. On the other hand, a few people, especially those who don't have many seizures, find the side effects make them feel worse than the epilepsy does, and so they choose not to take medication. In some cases, after trying a number of drugs without success, some people give up trying to find the 'right' medication.

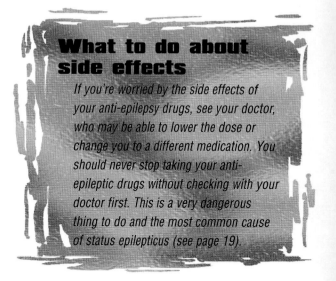

What to do about side effects

If you're worried by the side effects of your anti-epilepsy drugs, see your doctor, who may be able to lower the dose or change you to a different medication. You should never stop taking your anti-epileptic drugs without checking with your doctor first. This is a very dangerous thing to do and the most common cause of status epilepticus (see page 19).

Can epilepsy medication ever be stopped?

Sometimes epilepsy 'goes away' of its own accord. Doctors call this 'spontaneous remission' and this is when people are able to stop taking their anti-epileptic drugs without having any more seizures. Some children's epilepsy, for example, will stop by puberty, at around 12-14 years old.

It is often difficult to tell whether someone's epilepsy has stopped, so they have to be careful before stopping treatment altogether. Some doctors advise that if the person hasn't had a seizure for two or three years, then the drug can be gradually withdrawn. Others prefer to wait for five seizure-free years. Any anti-epileptic drug must be withdrawn gradually; for example, the person must take smaller and smaller doses over three to six months before stopping altogether.

'After two seizure-free years, I gradually came off medication. The hospital warned me the seizures might start again, but as they haven't so far – it's been 18 months – they say it's unlikely they'll come back now.' (Julie, aged 19)

There is around a 40 per cent chance that seizures will return after treatment is stopped. Usually, if this is going to happen, it will do so within the first few weeks or months, although it's possible for seizures to return after a year or more. If someone has still not had a seizure five years after stopping treatment, they are said to be in remission. Studies show that around 60-65 per cent of people are said to be in remission 10 years after being diagnosed with epilepsy. If seizures do return, treatment should be resumed.

Pill containers and drug wallets

It's hard to keep remembering to take your anti-epileptic drugs. Some people use pill containers or drug wallets that help them have the right amount of medication handy. The medication needs to be prepared beforehand, by putting the right amounts to be taken at different times in the different sections of the container.

'Andrew is 26, and has a mild learning disability. He shares a house with three others, and a social worker comes in daily. We've got him to remember to take his epilepsy medication by using a "pill reminder". So far, it's working well.' (Marion, mum)

Pill container
Some pill containers have compartments for each day of the week.

The use of brain surgery to treat epilepsy

Brain surgery may be considered in about five per cent of cases of epilepsy. If the epilepsy is caused by a specific problem in the brain, it may be possible for the surgeon to remove the damaged or abnormal part.

Doctors usually only consider surgery if all attempts at controlling seizures with medication have failed. This is because brain surgery is a major and very delicate operation, and there is a risk of damaging healthy parts of the brain. Anyone with epilepsy who wants surgery needs to undergo special tests to see if they are suitable for the

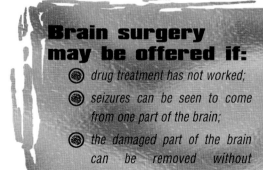

Brain surgery may be offered if:

- drug treatment has not worked;
- seizures can be seen to come from one part of the brain;
- the damaged part of the brain can be removed without damaging any other part;
- there are no other medical problems that would affect surgery.

operation. These tests are carried out at hospitals that have a specialist epilepsy department. They include brain scans and videotelemetry (see page 26), to find out the source of the epilepsy, and psychological tests to establish the location of the parts of the brain that control language, memory and movement. This is so that the surgeon can make sure that those parts are not damaged during surgery.

Surgery is completely successful for over 70 per cent of patients who undergo it, but for a small number there's no change or their epilepsy actually gets worse. Advances in MRI scanning (see page 26) mean it's becoming easier to find out exactly where in the brain a problem is occurring, and so surgery may become an increasingly popular option in the future.

Treatment by vagus nerve stimulation (VNS)

The vagus nerve in the neck carries information to and from the brain, and doctors think that it is connected to parts of the brain that may be involved in producing seizures. VNS is a fairly new technique. In an operation lasting 1-2 hours, a small pulse-generator is inserted into the patient's chest, just under the collarbone. A cable runs

Brain surgery
A patient undergoing brain surgery may be kept conscious, so that the surgeon can check that no damage is being done to the language, memory and movement parts of the brain.

from the generator to the vagus nerve. The generator is programmed to send out bursts of electricity to the nerve, disrupting epileptic activity by blocking the faulty messages that cause seizures. It runs on a special battery, which lasts for around 10 years and can be easily replaced under a general anaesthetic.

VNS is completely successful in around 15 per cent of cases. Most other people who undergo the procedure find the frequency of their seizures reduced by around 50 per cent over the next 18 months, with continuing improvement. For a small number of patients, VNS brings no improvement.

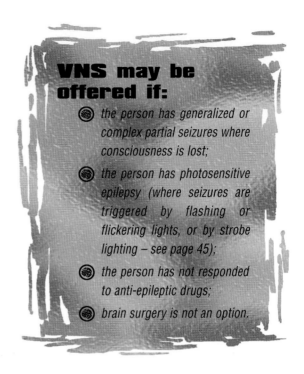

VNS may be offered if:

- ⊛ the person has generalized or complex partial seizures where consciousness is lost;
- ⊛ the person has photosensitive epilepsy (where seizures are triggered by flashing or flickering lights, or by strobe lighting – see page 45);
- ⊛ the person has not responded to anti-epileptic drugs;
- ⊛ brain surgery is not an option.

Complementary therapies

Complementary therapies are not meant to replace anti-epileptic drugs but to act as an extra treatment to help control epilepsy. These therapies are not subject to strict medical trials like conventional medicine, and there is still little evidence that many of them actually work. However, they may improve a person's sense of wellbeing and help them relax. Up to a third of people with epilepsy find that they have more seizures when they are stressed, so learning to relax can really help. The best complementary therapies for epilepsy seem to be those that relieve stress and promote relaxation, such as aromatherapy, massage or reflexology.

Anyone with epilepsy wanting to try a complementary therapy should always talk to their doctor first, to make sure that the therapy won't interfere with their epilepsy treatment. The complementary practioner also needs to know about their epilepsy and medication.

Stress relief
Massage can relieve stress, and this can reduce the likelihood of seizures.

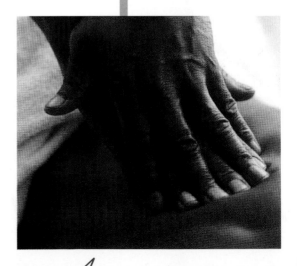

A treatment by diet

People with epilepsy don't need a special diet. As for everybody, it's important to eat healthily, which means plenty of fruit and vegetables as well as meals that are high in fibre and low in fat.

The 'ketogenic' diet has been used to try to control epilepsy in children. It is very strict and needs to be supervised by a hospital dietician. It consists mainly of fat, so it's not very tasty or healthy, and it doesn't always work. Even when it does, the effects may only last for a short time and anti-epileptic drugs usually have to be continued along with the diet. The diet can help a few children with very difficult epilepsy, but it's not suitable for the majority.

Seizure warning devices and dogs

Two new ideas to help people with epilepsy are based on the knowledge that the brain undergoes subtle changes before a seizure. Researchers are currently investigating the possibility of implanting a device in the brain that could give the person advance warning of a seizure, so that they could get to a safe place before it starts. This type of device could be linked to another implant which would be able to deliver a dose of an anti-epileptic drug or an electric impulse as soon as it detects the abnormal brain activity, thus preventing the seizure from happening.

'Seizure Alert dogs' are a similar idea, already in use. These are dogs that are trained to recognize when their owner is about to have a seizure (perhaps from a slight change in their natural scent, skin tone or eyes) and to react to this by circling the owner, pawing at the ground or barking. The owner then knows that they must get to a safe place where they can stay until the seizure is over. The dog stays with them during the seizure, and then receives a treat. Some dogs are specially trained before going to live with someone who needs their help. It is sometimes also possible to train the person's own dog.

'Mum knows she has 15 minutes to get out of danger once our dog Pip has warned her that a seizure's coming. When the seizure hits, Pip sits on her chest to stop her rocking around. Then he licks her face until she's OK again.' (Brett, aged 13)

5 How to make seizures less likely
Understanding the triggers

As shown in Chapter 4, taking anti-epileptic drugs is the main way of preventing seizures, or reducing their frequency. But, in addition, there are practical steps that people with epilepsy can take to make seizures less likely.

Identifying triggers

For most people who have epilepsy, seizures happen without warning. But some people might notice that their seizures happen at certain times or are triggered by something specific. For example, some people only have seizures while they are asleep, whereas others might find that watching television triggers a seizure. Keeping a diary of when seizures happen and the situations you are in at the time can help you work out what your particular triggers are. Then you can try to avoid the things you know may trigger a seizure. The diary is also helpful for the doctor who is monitoring your epilepsy. You can get special diaries from epilepsy charities (see page 62).

Keeping a record

A written record of when and where seizures occurred can be helpful in working out what triggers them.

Tiredness

Staying up late to watch TV or study for exams can trigger seizures in people with epilepsy, as can jet lag, shift work or just reading all night! Seizures are more likely when someone is very tired and has missed some sleep. If you have epilepsy, this doesn't mean that you have to be in bed early every night and that you cannot have a social life –

though staying out till 3am every weekend might not be such a good idea! Try to assess the level of tiredness at which you would be likely to have a seizure, and don't allow yourself to get that tired. Some people find that, as long as they don't stay out late more than two nights in a row, or as long as they catch up on sleep fairly regularly, they manage to stay seizure-free.

Emotional triggers

Everyone experiences stress at some point and it's not always a bad thing. But people may experience too much stress, and this can be a serious problem. People suffer from stress for many reasons. It may be due to worrying about exams, for example, or because a relationship has broken up. It could be caused by the death of someone close to them, or it may be that they have too much work or that they've lost their job. Being stressed, even when it doesn't seem to be serious, can trigger a seizure, so it's especially good for people with epilepsy to learn to relax.

Exam stress

'Sometimes I get seizures if I have a high temperature or a virus, but stress seems to be the biggest trigger of all. I took my GCSEs recently. I was really worried about how well I'd do, especially as I wanted to stay on at school and take A-levels. I was getting more and more stressed, and one day I had a seizure. It was the first time I'd had a seizure in years, as my medication usually controls them.

Now I have to really concentrate on not letting myself get so worried and stressed out. I love my dance classes and they really relax me, so I try not to miss one, even if I've got loads of homework. Also, when I feel myself getting anxious about something, I try to breathe slowly and stay calm. I don't worry too much about having seizures in future. As long as I don't let things get to me, I should be OK.'
(Sarah, aged 16)

Some people have seizures if they get angry or frustrated. As with stress, the most helpful answer is to find a way of managing feelings and preventing them from building up to an explosive level.

Boredom

Being bored is a form of stress that can also trigger seizures. When people are mentally active and enjoying what they are doing, they are far less likely to have a seizure. If you have epilepsy and find that boredom is a trigger, taking up a new interest can help. If you become really bored during school holidays, it might be an idea to join a club doing sports or other activities. You could also join a group through an epilepsy charity, so that you can meet and make friends with people in a similar situation.

Diet

Some people with epilepsy report having seizures when they are hungry. Doctors aren't really sure why this happens, although skipping meals and an unbalanced diet

Healthy eating
For everyone, it's best to eat at regular intervals and to learn to enjoy a healthy balance of different foods, with lots of fresh fruit and vegetables.

can lead to low sugar levels in the blood and this may be a trigger. Eating regular meals during the day does seem to help people with epilepsy to have fewer seizures. As for everyone, a balanced diet with plenty of fresh fruit and vegetables is important for general good health.

The effect of hormones

Some people develop epilepsy or find that their epilepsy goes away at a time in their life when their body goes through hormonal changes. This can happen during puberty, pregnancy or at the menopause (when a woman stops having periods, usually in her fifties). Some girls and women find that seizures are more likely or more frequent just before or during their period. If this happens, they should tell their doctor. It may be possible to increase medication in the week before their period, but this should only be done under the doctor's supervision.

'After keeping a seizure diary for five months, I realized that I have more seizures just before my period. My doctor advised me to take an increased dose of medication the week before I'm due on.'
(Chloe, aged 15)

How alcohol is a trigger

Alcohol is known to make seizures more likely, so people with epilepsy need to be particularly careful with drinking. Research suggests that drinking more than two units of alcohol (e.g. a pint of beer or two glasses of wine) can increase the risk of seizures, so someone with epilepsy should stick to an upper limit of two units. It may even be that this is too much. If someone has a seizure after drinking two units of alcohol, they should keep to one unit in future (as long as that doesn't trigger a seizure). Never be pressurized into drinking more than you want to. If you know someone with epilepsy, never encourage them to drink alcohol or to drink more than they want to.

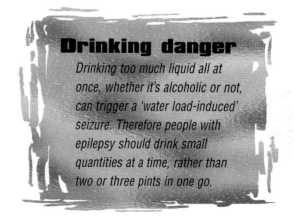

Drinking danger

Drinking too much liquid all at once, whether it's alcoholic or not, can trigger a 'water load-induced' seizure. Therefore people with epilepsy should drink small quantities at a time, rather than two or three pints in one go.

Withdrawal from alcohol can also trigger a seizure, so a seizure could happen while someone is out drinking or the

One of a crowd

'I'm not supposed to drink much because of my medication, and because too much alcohol could make me have a seizure. But it's tough not drinking when you're out with your mates. I usually join in and have a beer, but I have to be careful. Luckily, I sometimes get a warning that I'm going to have a seizure – my sense of smell changes and I get pins and needles in my head. When that happens, I try to go and lie down to sort myself out and recover. Occasionally, I feel down because I can't relax when I'm drinking. I still have a laugh with all the others, though, and if I'm honest, I'd rather stay sober and not have a seizure.'
(Luke, aged 22)

next day, as their body recovers from the effects of alcohol. Alcohol interacts with anti-epileptic drugs and can make them less effective, so that a seizure becomes more likely. The drugs can also make people more sensitive to the effects of alcohol, so they may get drunk and lose control sooner than their friends.

Recreational drugs and seizures

There is some evidence that illegal 'street' drugs, such as marijuana or cannabis, ecstasy, amphetamines, solvents, cocaine and heroin, can trigger seizures. Cocaine is known to trigger seizures even in people with no history of epilepsy, and in people with epilepsy it can make their seizures worse.

Taking drugs can also cause people to miss meals, not get enough sleep, or forget to take their anti-epileptic drugs. All these are factors that might make a seizure more likely.

Photosensitive epilepsy – triggered by lights

In some people with epilepsy, seizures can be triggered by flashing or flickering lights, such as the kind seen in nightclubs, called stroboscopic (strobe) lighting. Certain shapes and patterns may have the same effect, as can lots of different colours. This is called photosensitive epilepsy (PSE). It usually develops between the ages of seven and 19, but it's rare and only affects one in 10 people with epilepsy.

Strobe lighting strategies

People with PSE are usually advised to avoid situations such as nightclubs where they might encounter strobe lighting, but it's not always possible to know in advance. If strobe lighting does start up, cover one eye with the palm of your hand to cut down the number of brain cells stimulated by the flicker; then leave. This might feel silly, but it could prevent a seizure. Or you could try wearing light-responsive glasses with one lens treated so that it is totally darkened. The untreated lens stays clear so that you can see where you are going.

TV-induced seizures

An episode of **Pokemon**, broadcast on Japanese television in 1997, included a sequence of red and blue flashing lights. These triggered seizures in hundreds of people, mainly children. Doctors described this as a 'freak' occurrence, and said that, although some of the seizures were the result of photosensitive epilepsy, in many cases, the seizures were temporary in the same way that seizures sometimes result from a high fever.

As well as strobe lighting, the most common triggers for someone with PSE are:

- watching television;
- playing video games or using other computer graphics;
- seeing sunlight coming through a line of trees or flickering on water;
- looking out of the window of a fast-moving train.

If you have photosensitive epilepsy, watch the TV from at least two metres away and in a well-lit room. Use the remote control to switch channels, rather than go too close to the screen. Turn down the brightness on your VDU, or use an anti-glare screen. If you play video games, avoid playing if you are tired; take frequent breaks, and play in a well-lit room to reduce flicker. Playing with a patch over one eye may also help, as PSE depends on binocular ('both eyes') vision.

'My dad's always telling me off for sitting too close to the TV, and I've ended up having seizures a couple of times. He's right, but I just keep forgetting.'
(Marcus, aged 12)

Reducing the risk of epilepsy

In most cases of epilepsy the cause is unknown, and so there is nothing that can be done to prevent it completely. However, we do know that head injury and brain damage are the causes of some epilepsy. The risk of developing epilepsy can be reduced by taking care to avoid such injury and damage.

Anyone involved in activities such as horse-riding, cycling, boxing, riding a motorcycle or working on a construction site should protect their head by wearing the right headgear. Head injuries can also occur in road accidents, so protect yourself by following road safety rules and always wearing a seatbelt.

Damage to a baby's brain during pregnancy or birth can occur for several reasons. Sometimes it happens because the baby is born too early and cannot get enough oxygen because his or her lungs aren't fully developed. All pregnant women should take extra care during their pregnancies. We know, for example, that smoking while pregnant, although not directly linked with epilepsy, can cause babies to be born early, and this may mean they are more prone to brain damage. Drinking alcohol can also be harmful to the unborn baby, so ideally, pregnant women should have only an occasional alcoholic drink.

Headgear
You should always wear a helmet when cycling. A serious head injury can lead to epilepsy.

Important jabs

Some young children have non-epileptic seizures called febrile convulsions (see page 13). Occasionally these may happen after the child has had a jab to protect him or her against diseases such as tetanus, whooping cough, measles and mumps. Some parents worry that these jabs can lead to epilepsy and other health problems, but research shows that they are safe. It is important for children to be vaccinated against these diseases. Measles or whooping cough, for example, could cause brain damage and can even be fatal.

6 Living with epilepsy
How to deal with it

Being told that you have epilepsy can be very hard. It's normal to worry about how it will affect your life and about the side effects of any drugs you have to take. Other people may react differently to you at first; they may be scared that you will have a seizure when you are with them. It's important to remember that most people with epilepsy lead normal lives. Telling other people about the condition can help them, as well as you, to feel more at ease about it.

Depression and anxiety

Some people with epilepsy get depressed about having the condition. This means that they feel very sad for a long time, without being able to lift themselves out of their unhappiness. Depression like this can also be a side effect of anti-epileptic drugs, or it can be caused by the brain damage that resulted in epilepsy.

Anyone who feels sad or anxious for a long time can get advice from their doctor about sources of help. Counselling is available, and there are many social groups for people with epilepsy, where it can be helpful to share concerns. Anti-depressant drugs can be prescribed for someone who is very depressed, but the doctor needs to be careful that

Talking it over
If you can talk about epilepsy, it helps to get rid of people's worries and misunderstandings.

these will not interfere with anti-epileptic drugs. Some herbal treatments, such as St John's Wort, may help mild to moderate depression, but herbal remedies can also interact with anti-epileptic drugs, so their suitability needs to be checked with a doctor or pharmacist.

Warning signs

Some people's mood or behaviour changes before they have a seizure. Suddenly starting to feel miserable or worried for no apparent reason can be part of the warning or 'aura' that some people with epilepsy experience before a seizure.

Problems at home

All parents worry about their children because they care about them. So when a young person is diagnosed with epilepsy, it's not surprising that their parents worry even more. Everyone in the family needs to learn that, by taking a few precautions, people with epilepsy can lead an ordinary life and do most things that people without the condition can do.

Worries overcome

'We found out I had epilepsy when I was 12. It was a difficult time for me as I'd just started secondary school, I was getting interested in boys and felt I was growing up. My friends had started going out on their own – shopping or to the cinema – and I wanted to go with them, but Mum and Dad were always worried that I'd have a seizure while I was out and I'd get hurt or something. I told them it would be OK as long as I took my tablets, but they kept saying, "you might forget". We argued a lot. Then I got a MedicAlert bracelet which has brief details about my epilepsy and gives a number to phone to find out more. Mum and Dad also went into school to talk to the teachers about my epilepsy. This worked out well, because my form teacher told them she thought I was very sensible and she didn't think I was likely to forget my medication. They seemed much more relaxed after that, and they're fairly happy about me going out now.'
(Holly, aged 14)

Sometimes parents worry too much and become over-protective. They may be too anxious to let their children go out with their friends, go on holiday independently, or go clubbing. If you have epilepsy and you feel your parents are becoming over-protective, try to reassure them that you will always take your medication and do your best to avoid triggers. You could also ask your doctor or epilepsy nurse to have a chat with them about their concerns.

Safety around the home

Some people with epilepsy need to take safety precautions in and outside the home to avoid hurting themselves if they have a seizure. Those who are seizure-free with drugs, or who only have seizures in their sleep, need to take fewer precautions than those who may have seizures at any time without warning. Here are some simple tips, but if you or someone in your family has epilepsy, it's a good idea to get advice on safety from an epilepsy charity.

At home
Think about what would happen if someone had a seizure in different places around the home. What can be done to avoid them being injured?

- In the kitchen, it's safer to use a microwave than an ordinary cooker. You're less likely to get burnt if you have a seizure while cooking. If you do use an ordinary cooker, turn handles away from the front so that saucepans are not easily knocked over. When serving, take plates to the pan, not the other way around.

- In the bathroom, taking a shower is generally safer than having a bath. There is a risk of injury, however, so make sure the shower screen is made of plastic or safety glass. The bathroom door should open outwards, so that you wouldn't block the door if you fell. Try to shower when someone else is in the house, and always leave the door unlocked.

- In the living room, avoid open fires; if you have one, a secured fireguard must be fitted. Guards are also available for radiators. Make sure leads from electrical appliances don't trail across the floor.

- In the bedroom, if you tend to have seizures in your sleep, position the bed so that one side is against the wall. Place protective cushions around you and on the floor. This should help minimize the risk of injury from falling out of bed.

Problems at school

Some people with epilepsy are picked on at school. This may be because they lack confidence due to their epilepsy, or because the other kids see them as 'different'. But people with epilepsy are no different from anyone else. They just have a health problem to deal with, and most of the time they are fine. If you have epilepsy and you are bullied at school, try to talk about it with your parents or a teacher who can help sort out the problem. If you find this hard, you can talk in confidence to a counsellor at an epilepsy charity or a children's charity such as ChildLine (see page 62).

'Sometimes my epilepsy drugs affected my concentration, but the teachers understood and sorted out extra help when I needed it. I did well in my exams and now I'm looking forward to college.' (Brandon, aged 17)

Young people with epilepsy can achieve as much as any of their classmates. But sometimes epilepsy does affect schoolwork. Some people with epilepsy have poor attention, concentration problems, confusion, memory problems and tiredness. This may have something to do with the area of the brain that's damaged and causing the epilepsy; or it may be connected with anti-epileptic medication, which can affect concentration and cause fatigue. It's important for teachers to know about the person's epilepsy, especially about any problems with tiredness or poor concentration, so that extra help can be given if necessary. Teachers also need to know what type of seizures the student may have, and what needs to be done if a seizure occurs. In most cases the young person can return to class after they've rested and had some time to recover.

Most young people with epilepsy go to ordinary schools and colleges, and can take part in most activities. Some children with epilepsy have a learning disability, which means they find it harder to do schoolwork than someone else of the same age. These children need special help with their studies. They may go to a 'special school', or get extra support from a special needs tutor in an ordinary school.

Going to college or university

Carrying on your studies at college or university can help your career and social life, and help you develop as a person. If you have epilepsy, it is something extra to keep in mind when you are choosing what course to do and where to do it.

Branching out
Going to college or university often means living away from home for the first time. You may need to bear your epilepsy in mind when you are arranging your accommodation.

Young people choose college or university courses for different reasons. They may choose a subject in which they have a special interest, or a subject that will lead them towards a particular job or career. Careers officers can offer advice. If you have epilepsy, you can also get help from organizations like the National Bureau for Students with Disabilities (see page 62). When choosing a course, and thinking about the career that it will lead to, remember that some jobs are restricted if you have epilepsy.

If you have epilepsy and are choosing a university or college, it's probably a good idea to find out if the college has experience of teaching students with epilepsy – some may be used to allowing extra time for exams, or they may have special computers for people with photosensitive epilepsy. Some might give priority to students with epilepsy when allocating accommodation on campus.

Work and careers

Nearly all jobs are open to people with epilepsy. However, when thinking of a possible career, if you have epilepsy, you'll need to consider the type of seizures you have, how often they occur, how controlled they are, and how they might affect your work.

'I was worried about applying for teacher training because of my epilepsy, but they said they assess each case individually. I think it's to do with health and safety. I've been accepted and I start in September!'
(Marcus, aged 21)

A few jobs are barred by law in the UK to people with any history of epilepsy. Others have restrictions – for example, they may only be open to those who have had no seizures since the age of five. In the UK, people with epilepsy are not allowed to be aircraft pilots, ambulance drivers, fire-fighters, merchant seamen or train drivers. In careers such as the police force, prison service and armed forces, there are a number of restrictions and some areas are completely barred to those with epilepsy. This is because having a seizure while working could put the person themselves or others at risk of injury or death.

However, this doesn't necessarily mean that your dream job is out of the question. Many of these jobs have specific regulations, according to which someone with epilepsy may be admitted if they have not had any seizures for many years. The rules would need to be checked with the relevant employer.

In the UK, anyone who has epilepsy and is looking for a job can get help from a Disability Employment Helpline, run by the Employment Service. The Helpline number and more information are available from local Job Centres. If you have epilepsy, you must by law tell your employer. However, it is not necessary to put this information on a job application form unless it is specifically asked for. Although employers must not discriminate against people who have epilepsy, some people feel that they have a better chance of getting an interview if the employer doesn't know in advance about their epilepsy.

Helping employers understand

'I work most weekends and holidays in a garage. I love working on engines, and it gives me some extra money while I'm finishing my exams. I was worried about telling my boss, Ken, that I had epilepsy, because some people think it means you can't do a job like this. He was funny about it at first, but he admitted it was because he didn't know much about it. I followed some advice from an epilepsy group and wrote down all the details of my epilepsy, especially that I'm on medication, so I don't get many seizures these days, and that I always know when there's one coming. I've only had one seizure at work, but I got this weird feeling in my stomach and I knew what was happening. I told Ken, and he went a bit pale, but he knew what to expect and I told him not to worry. He let me go into his office, and even let me lie on the floor to rest afterwards. He understands it now, so he's fine. In fact, I sometimes think he wants me to have another seizure, just so he can prove to me how cool he is about it!'
(Lee, aged 18)

Driving

There are restrictions on driving for people with epilepsy, but having the condition doesn't mean that you cannot ever drive. To apply for a driving licence, a person with epilepsy has to have been seizure-free for 12 months or to have had seizures only during their sleep for at least three years.

If someone with a driving licence has a seizure, even if they have not been diagnosed as having epilepsy, they must tell the Driver and Vehicle Licensing Authority (DVLA) and stop driving immediately. Anyone who doesn't inform the DVLA and continues to drive is breaking the law and will not be insured to drive. After stopping driving because of a seizure, the person has to be seizure-free for 12 months before they can apply for a licence again.

People withdrawing from anti-epileptic drugs have an increased risk of having a seizure, so someone coming off the drugs should not drive during this time or for six months afterwards. All these rules sound very harsh, but they are important for everyone's safety.

Traffic

If someone had a seizure while driving, the consequences could be very serious. Therefore the law about this needs to be strict.

'I've had seizures in the last year so I can't learn to drive yet. It's frustrating, especially as all my mates are learning. My doctor is going to try me on different drugs.'
(Ashley, aged 18)

Sports and leisure

Having epilepsy doesn't mean that you cannot take part in lots of sport and leisure activities, but it is wise to think about your epilepsy and take precautions against possible dangers. What type of epilepsy is it? How often do seizures occur? What are the side effects of any drugs you take? Do you need supervision when you are taking part in the activity? It's a good idea to do sports and other activities with a friend who knows what to do if you have a seizure. It's also important to tell the leader or supervisor about your condition. Avoid going a long time without food and drink, and getting too hot or cold, as these things can trigger seizures.

Sports precautions

Swimming

Having a seizure in water means you could drown. Wear a life-belt, go with a friend and tell the pool attendant or lifeguard that you have epilepsy.

Climbing

Never climb alone. Go with a group, and have a safety plan in case you have a seizure.

Horse-riding

Always wear a riding helmet and avoid riding alone.

Cycling

Wear a safety helmet. Avoid cycling on public roads if your seizures aren't well controlled. Avoid cycling alone.

Diving

Someone having a seizure while under water could bite through or let go of the valve or mouthpiece to their breathing apparatus. Also, breathing speeds up during a seizure, so the body demands oxygen at a faster rate than the valve can supply it. This means the person could black out through lack of oxygen. Diving experts advise that you need to have been seizure-free and off medication for five years.

Contact sports

Activities such as rugby, football and hockey should be fine, but if your epilepsy was caused by a head injury your doctor might advise you against playing these sports.

Going on holiday

When people with epilepsy go on holiday, they need to take some precautions and let people know about their condition. For someone who has regular seizures, it's best to let the travel company know when booking the holiday, and to let the flight crew know on the plane. There may be some difficulty in getting travel insurance, but there are companies that have policies designed for people with epilepsy. Epilepsy charities can put you in touch with them.

'I was panicking before the holiday, but Mum helped me make a list. It covered everything – with tick boxes! On the day I was relaxed and well prepared – the holiday was fantastic. I just needed to get organized.'
(Emma, aged 17)

If you have epilepsy and are going abroad, make sure you take enough of your anti-epileptic drugs with you, and keep them in the right packaging so that there is no problem explaining if you are stopped by customs. Also, make sure you keep them in your hand luggage, rather than packing them in your suitcase. That way, if there was a problem such as long delays, or if your suitcases went missing, at least you would have your medication with you. Talk to your doctor about any travel worries before you go.

On holiday with epilepsy?

You can enjoy your holiday to the full, if you are prepared and have taken the necessary precautions.

Love and marriage

When a couple fall in love and one or both of them has epilepsy, they may worry about how the condition will affect their relationship and their future together. They may be concerned that epilepsy will affect their ability to have children.

Some research suggests that epilepsy and its treatment may affect fertility. Other studies show no difference in fertility rates between people who have epilepsy and people who don't. Normally, epilepsy should not stop someone having a family, although women with epilepsy should seek their doctor's advice about this. Drug levels and frequency of seizures need to be monitored throughout pregnancy, to protect the health of mother and baby. The mother must not stop taking anti-epileptic drugs during her pregnancy, as major convulsions such as a tonic-clonic seizure could harm the baby or lead to miscarriage. There is a slight risk of birth defects, such as spina bifida, in babies born to women taking anti-epileptic drugs.

'I was worried that I would pass my epilepsy on to any children I might have. The doctor explained that, even if a child of mine did inherit a gene that could cause epilepsy, the child would not necessarily develop the condition.' (Jo)

Talking about epilepsy

It can be hard to tell people that you have epilepsy. However, talking about it, especially to people you spend a lot of time with, is better than keeping it a secret. That way, people become used to the idea and less nervous of witnessing a seizure. They could help you if you have one. Hopefully, they will also see that epilepsy is just a small part of you and that you have a normal life like anyone else.

If you have a friend or relative with epilepsy, you can help them by learning more about the condition. Find out what their particular triggers are and don't encourage them to do things like drinking too much or staying out late if these are problems for them.

Some famous people with epilepsy

Agatha Christie	Neil Young
Richard Burton	Jonty Rhodes
Elton John	Tony Grieg
Rick Mayall	Margaret McEleney
Hugo Weaving	(Paralympic medallist)

The way ahead

Planning your way ahead in life is always complicated, but when you have a health condition that can affect your choices, it can be even more of a puzzle.
Understanding epilepsy can help you to make the right decisions about your future.

Looking forward

Continuing research into drug treatment and surgery means that the outlook for people with epilepsy is improving. Currently, up to 80 per cent of people with epilepsy will eventually stop having seizures. But whether someone stops having seizures altogether, has fewer seizures as they get older, or continues to have seizures for the rest of their life, epilepsy need not stop them having an enjoyable and productive life. Most people with epilepsy have very normal and ordinary lives. Others have lives that could be described as 'extraordinary', achieving things that many of us only dream about. They include great statesmen, philosophers, writers, poets, actors, sportspeople, comedians, popstars and artists. If you or someone you know has epilepsy, it may be worrying at first, but by making use of the vast range of information available, you can understand the condition and its treatment, so that it becomes much easier to live with.

Glossary

ambulatory monitoring a portable type of EEG (see below). It allows brainwaves to be recorded while the person is going about their day-to-day life.

aromatherapy a complementary therapy involving the use of aromatic (scented) oils for massage or inhalation.

aura a warning, usually in the form of a strange sensation, smell or taste, that a seizure is about to happen.

automatism strange action or behaviour carried out while someone is having a seizure.

CAT or CT scan (computed tomography) a brain scan that uses X-rays to produce images representing 'slices' of the brain.

cerebrum the largest part of the brain, made up of two halves or 'cerebral hemispheres'.

complementary therapies non-medical treatments (e.g. aromatherapy) which can be used as well as conventional treatments.

convulsion another name for a seizure, usually describing violent movements.

EEG a test that records the electrical signals produced in the brain. A machine called an electro-encephalo*graph* picks up the information and transfers it to a computer to produce an image or 'trace' of the brain patterns. This is called an electroencephalo*gram*.

electrode small disc placed on the head during an EEG to pick up brainwaves and transfer them through the attached wires to the EEG machine.

fertility the capability of reproduction.

gene part of a human cell that contains certain traits or characteristics that can be passed from generation to generation.

genetic carried or passed on through the genes.

grand mal an old-fashioned name (though still used by some) for tonic-clonic seizures. It is a French phrase, meaning 'great illness'. Nowadays people don't think this is an appropriate description of epilepsy and so the term is falling out of use.

hemisphere one of the two parts of the cerebrum, the largest part of the brain.

hormonal change a change in the levels of hormones (chemical messengers) in a person's blood. This can happen at certain times in life, for example at puberty, during pregnancy or at the menopause (when a woman stops having periods).

hyper-ventilation breathing too fast and too hard. This overbreathing may trigger a seizure, so is sometimes deliberately brought on during an EEG so that an accurate recording of abnormal brainwaves can be made.

learning disability where someone's intellectual ability does not develop as normal. This can affect speech, reading, writing, co-ordination and behaviour. In mild cases, there may be no obvious cause, but more severe learning disabilities are often due to birth defects, brain damage or genetic disorders.

lobe	one of the areas that make up the cerebral hemispheres in the brain. There are four lobes – frontal, occipital, parietal and temporal – in each of the two hemispheres. Each lobe controls specific functions of the body.
metabolize	to break down or 'process' substances such as food or medicines.
MRI (magnetic resonance imaging)	a type of brain scan, more detailed than a CT scan, which uses magnetism to produce images of the brain.
nausea	feeling sick.
neurological	to do with the brain and nervous system.
neurone	a nerve cell that transmits electrical impulses.
neuro-transmitter	a chemical released in the brain, creating an electrical message that can pass between the neurones.
petit mal	literally 'little illness' in French. An old-fashioned term for absence seizures.
pseudo-seizures	seizures that resemble epileptic seizures, but which are not caused by epilepsy. They are real seizures, but may have a psychological cause. Sometimes called 'non-epileptic seizures'.
recovery position	a safe, 'first aid' position for someone who is unconscious. The position keeps the back and neck aligned and the airways open, and allows fluid to drain from the mouth should the person vomit.
reflexology	a complementary therapy involving massage of the feet. The technique is based on the idea that energy is channelled from parts of the foot to other specific parts of the body.
seizure	sudden, uncontrolled bursts of abnormal electrical activity in the brain resulting in a change in behaviour, involuntary movements, loss of consciousness or a combination of these.
seizure threshold	the level at which someone will have a seizure. E.g. Anti-epileptic drugs may raise the threshold; lack of sleep may lower it.
spina bifida	a birth defect which, in more severe cases, causes part of the spinal cord to be completely exposed. Less serious cases may result in a minor abnormality of the vertebrae.
spontaneous remission	when an illness gets better on its own. In epilepsy, this is where seizures have stopped and drug treatment is no longer needed.
status epilepticus	a seizure lasting more than 30 minutes, or several seizures, one after the other, which last that long in total, without the person regaining consciousness in between.
stroke	damage to the brain caused by an interruption in the blood supply.
syndrome	where several signs and symptoms occur together to make up a particular condition.
video-telemetry	a test where a video camera is linked to an EEG machine, in order to record how a person's activities affect their seizures.

Resources

Useful organizations

British Epilepsy Association
Anstey House, 40 Hanover Square, Leeds LS3 1BE
Telephone: 0113 243 9393   Helpline: 0800 309030
www.epilepsy.org

ChildLine
Helpline: 0800 1111
24-hour helpline for children and young people with
any type of problem.

Headway
(National Head Injuries Association Limited)
47 King Edward Court, King Edward Street,
Nottingham NG1 1EW
Telephone: 0115 924 0800
Provides support and advice for people who have
suffered head injury.

International Bureau for Epilepsy
PO Box 21, 3100 AA Heemstede, The Netherlands
Telephone: 00 3123 5291019   Email: ibe@xs40all.nl
Provides details of epilepsy associations throughout
the world.

MENCAP
Mencap National Centre, 123 Golden Lane,
London EC1 0RT
Telephone: 020 7454 0454
Provides advice and support for people with learning
disabilities and their families.

National Society for Epilepsy
Chalfont Centre for Epilepsy,
Chalfont St Peter, Bucks SL9 0RJ
Telephone: 01494 601300   www.epilepsynse.org.uk

SCOPE
6 Market Road, London N7 9PW
Helpline: 0800 626216
Provides information and counselling service on
cerebral palsy and associated disabilities; also runs
schools and residential centres for people with
cerebral palsy.

SKILL
(National Bureau for Students with Disabilities)
18-29 Crucifix Lane, London SE1 3JW
Telephone: 020 7450 0620

St Piers
St Pier's Lane, Lingfield, Surrey RH7 6PW
Telephone: 01342 832243
Provides assessment and long-term care and
education for children and young adults with severe
epilepsy and learning difficulties.

Identification Jewellery is available from:

MedicAlert Foundation, 1 Bridge Wharf,
156 Caledonian Road, London N1 9UU
(Telephone: 020 7833 3034)

Golden Key, 1 Hare Street, Sheerness,
Kent ME12 1AH (Telephone: 01795 663403)

SOS Talisman, Talman Ltd, 21 Grays Corner,
Ley Street, Ilford, Essex IG2 7RQ
(Telephone: 020 8554 5579)

Further information

The Illustrated Junior Encyclopaedia of Epilepsy,
editor Dr Richard Appleton (Petroc Press, 1996)
Aimed mainly at 9-14 year-olds, but of interest to
anyone with a connection to epilepsy.

Putting you in the picture, a video suitable for all
the family. Presented by Rolf Harris. Available from
NSE online shop.

The Lost Prince (DVD), BBC, 2003. The true story of a
royal child, hidden away because of his epilepsy.

Disclaimer
The website addresses (URLs) included in this book were
valid at the time of going to press. However, because of the
nature of the internet, it is possible that some addresses
may have changed, or sites may have changed or closed
down since publication. While the author and the
publishers regret any inconvenience this may cause readers,
no responsibility for any such changes can be accepted by
either the author or the publishers.

Index